Country Explorers

TANZANIA

Anna Cavallo

Lerner Publications Company • Minneapolis

Lerner Publications Company
A division of Lerner Publishing Group, Inc.
241 First Avenue North
Minneapolis, MN 55401 U.S.A.

Website address: www.lernerbooks.com

Library of Congress Cataloging-in-Publication Data

Cavallo, Anna.
    Tanzania / by Anna Cavallo.
        p.   cm. — (Country explorers)
    Includes index.
    ISBN 978–0–7613–6411–5 (lib. bdg. : alk. paper)
    1. Tanzania—Juvenile literature. I. Title.
DT438.C38 2011
967.8—dc22   2010018958

Manufactured in the United States of America
1 – VI – 12/31/10

Table of Contents

Welcome!

We're heading to Tanzania! This country lies in eastern Africa. Kenya and Uganda sit to the north. West of Tanzania are Rwanda, Burundi, and the Democratic Republic of Congo. To the south, you'll find Zambia, Malawi, and Mozambique. The islands of Zanzibar are part of Tanzania too.

The Indian Ocean washes Tanzania's eastern coast. Three big lakes also touch Tanzania. Lake Victoria is the world's second-largest lake. It lies in the north. Lake Tanganyika sits to the west. It is the second-deepest lake in the world. Lake Nyasa hugs Tanzania's southwest border.

equator

Tanzania

The Indian Ocean washes up along the coast of Zanzibar.

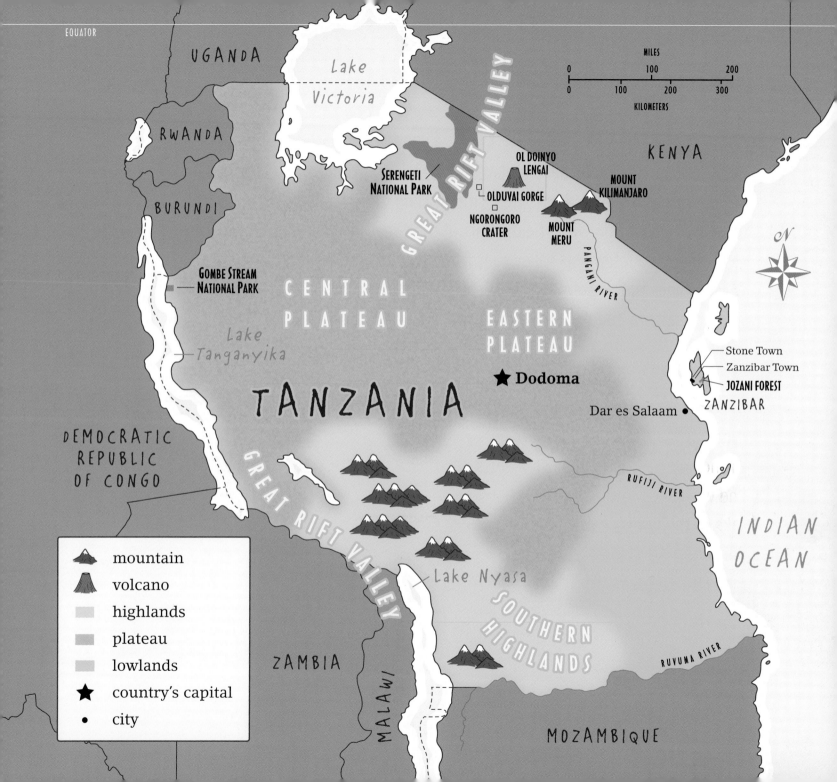

EQUATOR

UGANDA

Lake Victoria

RWANDA

KENYA

BURUNDI

GREAT RIFT VALLEY

Serengeti National Park

OL DOINYO LENGAI

OLDUVAI GORGE

MOUNT KILIMANJARO

NGORONGORO CRATER

MOUNT MERU

Gombe Stream National Park

CENTRAL PLATEAU

EASTERN PLATEAU

PANGANI RIVER

Lake Tanganyika

N

DEMOCRATIC REPUBLIC OF CONGO

★ Dodoma

Stone Town
Zanzibar Town
JOZANI FOREST
ZANZIBAR

Dar es Salaam ●

TANZANIA

GREAT RIFT VALLEY

RUFIJI RIVER

INDIAN OCEAN

MILES

0   100   200

0   100   200   300

KILOMETERS

Lake Nyasa

SOUTHERN HIGHLANDS

🏔 mountain

🌋 volcano

highlands

plateau

lowlands

★ country's capital

● city

ZAMBIA

MALAWI

RUVUMA RIVER

MOZAMBIQUE

The Land

High, flat land called a plateau covers central Tanzania. Savannas are flat, grassy areas. They stretch across much of this area. Short trees dot the wide fields. Part of the Great Rift Valley cuts through the country. This valley runs from north to south. Another part lines the western border. Beaches and low coastline form the eastern edge of the country.

Part of the Great Rift Valley contains a chain of mountains and volcanoes.

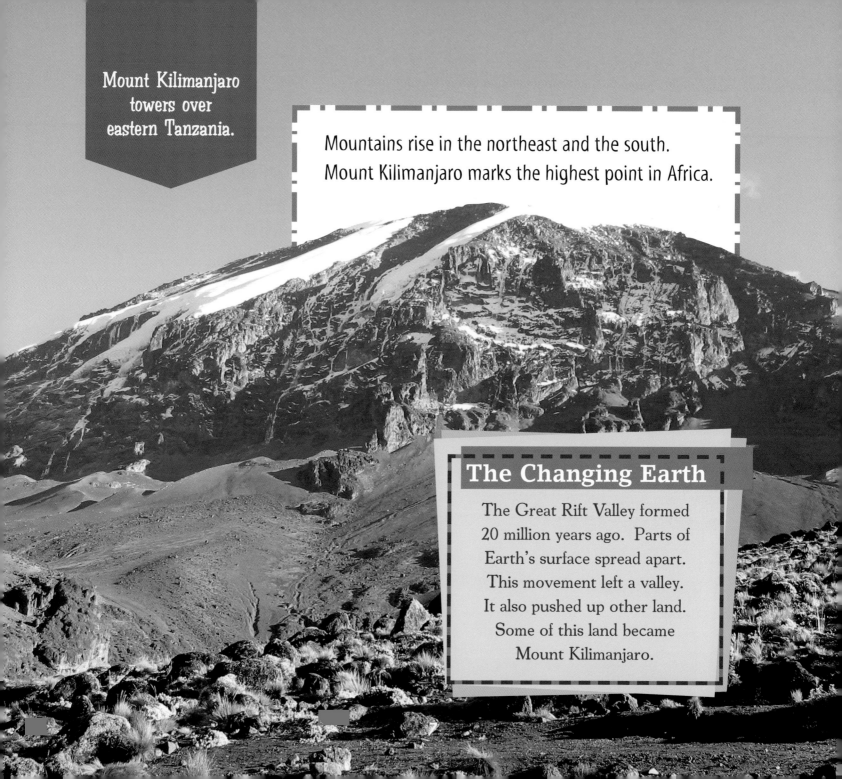

Mount Kilimanjaro towers over eastern Tanzania.

Mountains rise in the northeast and the south. Mount Kilimanjaro marks the highest point in Africa.

The Changing Earth

The Great Rift Valley formed 20 million years ago. Parts of Earth's surface spread apart. This movement left a valley. It also pushed up other land. Some of this land became Mount Kilimanjaro.

Zanzibar

Sandy beaches and palm trees line the islands of Zanzibar. These islands are a popular vacation spot. Stone Town is part of Zanzibar Town, the main city. Its beautiful old buildings include palaces and mosques. Mosques are Islamic places of worship.

Coconut palm trees line the shore of Zanzibar.

Zanzibar is famous for the coconuts and cloves and other spices that grow there. Fish are another island specialty. People catch and eat them. People also like to watch them under water.

Map Whiz Quiz

Take a look at the map on page 5. Trace the outline of Tanzania onto a sheet of paper. Don't forget Zanzibar! Can you find the Indian Ocean? Mark it with an *E* for east. Then color it blue. What about Kenya? Mark it with an *N* for north. Find Burundi, and give it a *W* for west. Then label Mozambique with an *S* for south.

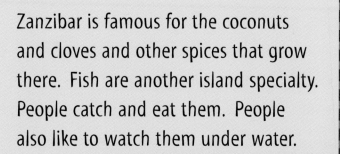

Many people go diving off Zanzibar's coast.

Wildlife Safari

Tanzania is the perfect place for a safari (wildlife trip)!
Elephants, giraffes, lions, wildebeests, gazelles, zebras,
leopards, and many other animals roam the land.
More than one thousand kinds of birds live there.

African elephants
graze the land near
Mount Kilimanjaro.

National parks and wildlife reserves cover about one-fourth of the country. Animals living in them are protected from hunters. Serengeti National Park is the country's oldest wildlife reserve. The park is a popular spot for tourists.

Dear Liz,

You won't believe what I've seen! Today we went to Ngorongoro Crater. The huge crater was once a volcano. Then its top caved in. That formed a crater miles wide. Tons of animals live inside the crater. I saw a black rhino, some elephants, and a leopard!

See you soon,
Sara

Ngorongoro Crater

How's the Weather?

Most of Tanzania is warm and pleasant all year. Zanzibar and the coast are usually hot and humid. The inner plains cool off at night. The mountains can be much colder.

Giraffes like northern Tanzania, where the weather is warm.

From October to April, the weather is warmer than between May and September. But the seasons don't change much. Most rain falls between November and May.

Tanzanian Time

The sun always rises at 6:00 A.M. in Tanzania. And it always sets at 6:00 P.M. Tanzanians tell time by counting the hours since the sunrise or sunset. This system is called Swahili time. (Swahili is one of Tanzania's languages.) So 7:00 A.M. is 1:00 Swahili time, because it is one hour after sunrise!

The sky is shades of purple, pink, and orange during a sunset.

Early Humans to Independence

Some of the first humans on Earth lived in Tanzania two million years ago. Scientists think these early people later traveled to other parts of Africa and to other continents.

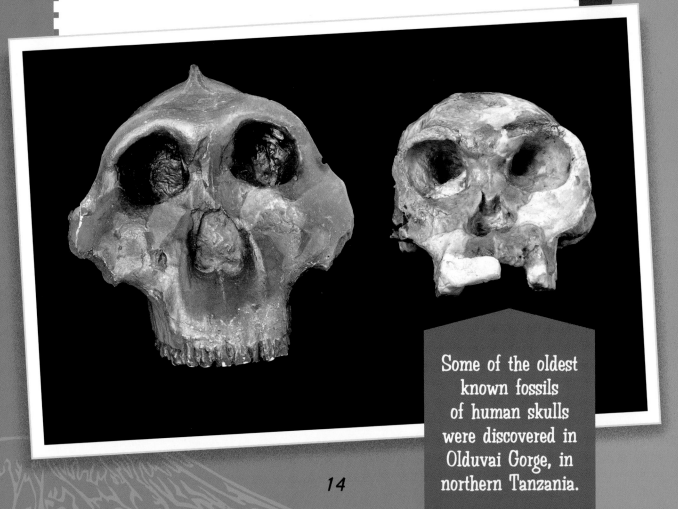

Some of the oldest known fossils of human skulls were discovered in Olduvai Gorge, in northern Tanzania.

By 1840, Arabs had moved to Zanzibar. They came from the Middle East. The Arabs traded pottery and cloth for African spices, gold, and ivory. European explorers arrived in eastern Africa about 1850. Modern-day Tanzania was under the rule of Germany and then Great Britain for many years. Tanzania finally gained independence in 1964. The mainland and Zanzibar joined as one nation.

Jakaya Mrisho Kikwete, Tanzania's president in 2010, holds up a spear and a shield painted in the country's national colors.

Modern People

The people of Tanzania belong to more than 130 ethnic groups! Nearly all are African. The Sukuma make up the largest group with 14 percent of the population. Other major groups are the Haya, the Nyamwezi, the Makonde, and the Swahili. One in one hundred Tanzanians is European, Asian, or Arabian. Most of the country's Arabs live in Zanzibar.

Sukuma people dance in Bujora, a village in northern Tanzania.

Masai men leap high in the air during a traditional jumping dance. The dance displays their strength.

The Masai

The Masai live in northern Tanzania. These cattle herders lead a traditional way of life. They live in simple homes. The Masai build the walls with mud and poles or sticks. They use thatch or mud to make the roof. Masai people mainly depend on milk and food from their herds. In recent years, some Masai have moved to cities to get jobs. Disease and lack of rain have made it harder to keep and feed cattle.

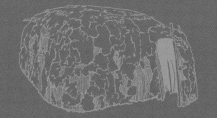

Dar es Salaam

Tanzania's largest city is Dar es Salaam. This crowded port city sits on the Indian Ocean. Local people just call it Dar.

Modern skyscrapers stand alongside older buildings on the coast of Dar es Salaam.

Students take notes during a lecture at Dar es Salaam University.

Dar is a center of business and culture. People come to enjoy its markets, restaurants, museums, beaches, and historic buildings. Dar also has several universities.

Dodoma

Dar es Salaam was Tanzania's first capital. In 1974, the capital moved to Dodoma. This small city lies in the central highlands. The law-making body of the government meets here. But the president and other parts of the government haven't moved yet. They are still based in Dar es Salaam.

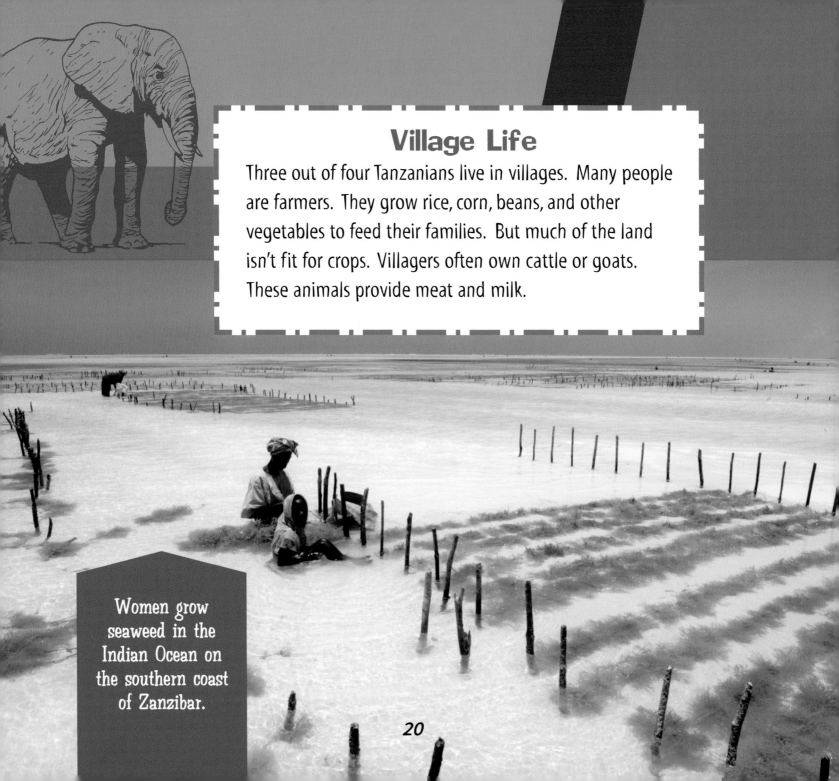

Village Life

Three out of four Tanzanians live in villages. Many people are farmers. They grow rice, corn, beans, and other vegetables to feed their families. But much of the land isn't fit for crops. Villagers often own cattle or goats. These animals provide meat and milk.

Women grow seaweed in the Indian Ocean on the southern coast of Zanzibar.

Women carry water in big calabashes in the Dodoma area in central Tanzania.

Daily life in villages involves a lot of work. Women must walk to a well, a pond, or a river to get water. They may have to walk a long way to find water during the dry season. Women also tend the fields, cook, and watch the children. Men farm, care for animals, and hunt and fish.

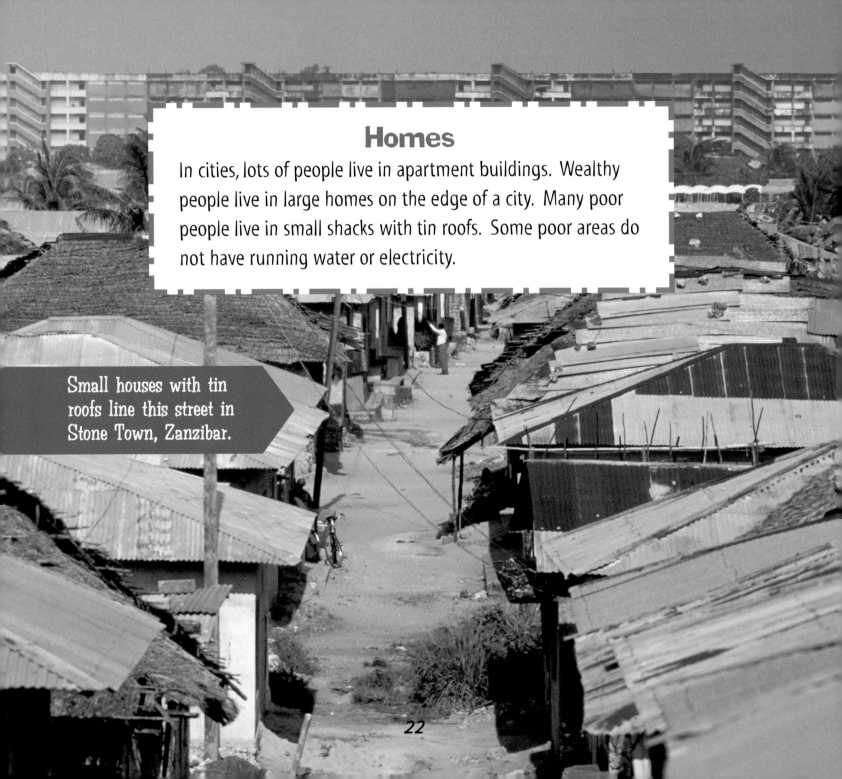

Homes

In cities, lots of people live in apartment buildings. Wealthy people live in large homes on the edge of a city. Many poor people live in small shacks with tin roofs. Some poor areas do not have running water or electricity.

Small houses with tin roofs line this street in Stone Town, Zanzibar.

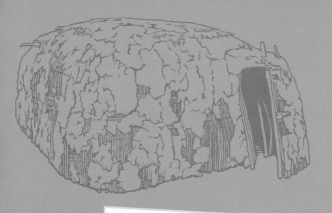

In villages, people live in small houses. Grandparents, parents, and children often live together. Grandparents help raise the children.

This family of women and children lives together in a brick house.

Transportation

Getting around can be an adventure. For a ride in the city, hop on a *dala dala*. These are vans, minibuses, or trucks. They carry people along a certain route. But don't expect to have much room! Dala dalas are usually crowded.

A dala dala full of people passes an old train station.

People walk and ride their bicycles near a market.

Many people walk or ride bicycles to get around. Wealthy people have cars. To travel between towns, most Tanzanians take buses.

Food

Hungry? People in Tanzania eat a lot of rice and corn. They make a porridge from corn. This dish is called *ugali*. Meals often include ugali or rice and goat meat, fish, beef, or chicken. Lunch is usually the biggest meal. Breakfast may just be coffee or tea and bread.

Ugali is often part of a meal in Tanzania.

Many vegetables and fruits grow well in Tanzania. People can enjoy fresh avocados, spinach, pineapples, and bananas. In fact, at least seventeen kinds of bananas grow in this country! People eat them fresh, fried, in stew, and dried.

A banana market stays busy in the village of Mwika in northeastern Tanzania.

Markets

Most people don't go to a grocery store. Instead, they buy their food at markets. They talk with the seller to get the best price.

27

Religion

About one out of three Tanzanians are Christian. About the same number are Muslim (followers of Islam). These Tanzanians dress more modestly than others. Islamic children study the Koran, the Muslim holy book, as well as their schoolwork.

Muslim children make their way home from school.

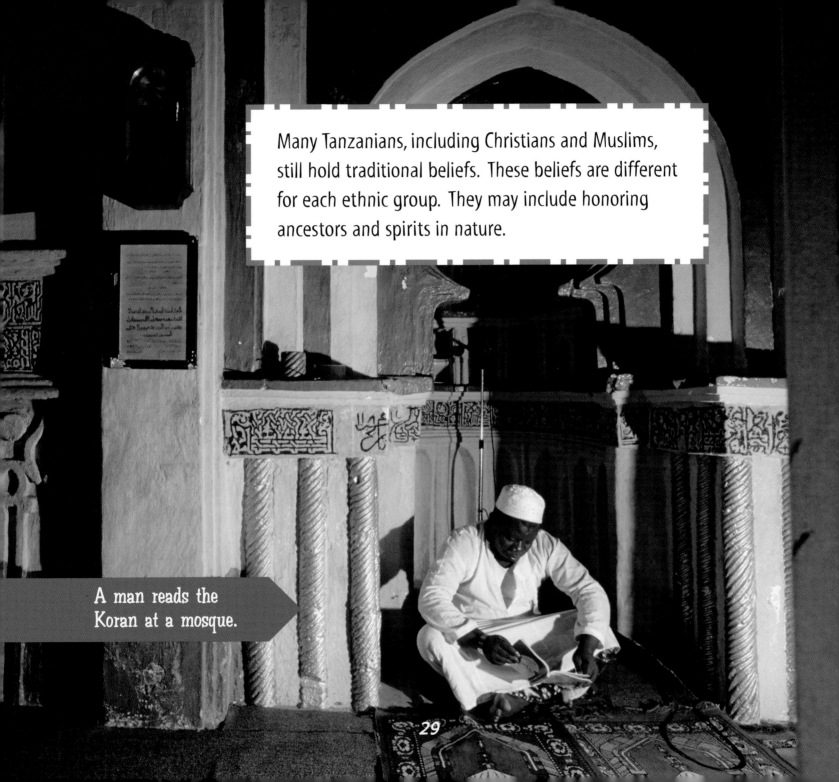

Many Tanzanians, including Christians and Muslims, still hold traditional beliefs. These beliefs are different for each ethnic group. They may include honoring ancestors and spirits in nature.

A man reads the Koran at a mosque.

Language

More than 120 languages are spoken in Tanzania! Almost everyone speaks Swahili. This language brings together words from other languages. These include Arabic, English, and Bantu. Most people speak at least one other language too.

A stand in Dar es Salaam sells newspapers in English and Swahili.

Speaking Swahili

Here are some useful words and sayings in Swahili.

English	Swahili	(How to say it)
hello	jambo	(JAHM-boh)
How are you?	Habani?	(hah-BAH-nee)
good	nzuri	(un-ZOO-ree)
please	tafadhali	(TAH-fuh-DAH-lee)
thank you very much	asante sana	(uh-SAHN-teh SAH-nuh)
I'm very sorry.	Pole sana.	(POH-leh SAH-nuh)
yes	ndiyo	(un-DEE-yoh)
no	hapana	(hah-PAH-nah)

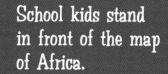

School kids stand in front of the map of Africa.

Time for School

Kids in Tanzania go to primary school for seven years. Classes are taught in Swahili. Students take a big test when they finish primary school. Some students go on to four or six years of secondary school. Classes there are in English.

Children study in a classroom in south central Tanzania.

Students wear their school uniforms.

What do you wear to school? Kids in Tanzania wear uniforms. Families have to pay for uniforms, school supplies, and national tests. Children in secondary school have to pay for tuition (the cost to attend school) and books too. All these costs make school too expensive for many people.

Economy

Farming makes up the biggest part of the economy. Tanzania sells its coffee, tea, cotton, spices, and bananas around the world. Mining diamonds and gold is also an important industry.

This woman is picking cotton on a farm.

Tourism is another important business. Tourists flock to Tanzania for wildlife safaris. They also visit Dar es Salaam, Zanzibar, and other spots.

Elephants cross the path of tourists on a safari.

Celebrations

Festivals are big, joyful events in Tanzania. People travel long distances to join in a family celebration. Many ethnic groups hold coming-of-age ceremonies. These honor a child who is becoming an adult.

A Masai warrior wears traditional face paint during a coming-of-age ceremony.

Tanzanians also observe national holidays. April 26 is Union Day. That's the day Tanzania formed a united country with Zanzibar. The Christian holidays Easter and Christmas are national holidays. So is the Muslim festival Eid al-Fitr, a time of feasting after the end of the holy month of Ramadan.

Villagers in southern Tanzania celebrate Eid al-Fitr with music and dance.

Kids play drums
and dance
together outside.

Music

Tanzania has a rich history of
music. Drums, singing, and dancing
are often part of village events.
Different drums, rattles, thumb
pianos, and flutes create many
rhythms and melodies.

38

Young people listen to hip-hop, rap, and reggae music on the radio. American and other foreign artists are popular. Many Tanzanian musicians play hip-hop and dance music too. A style of sung Swahili poetry, called *taarab*, combines Indian and Arab styles with African music.

A Masai man listens to music on a boom box.

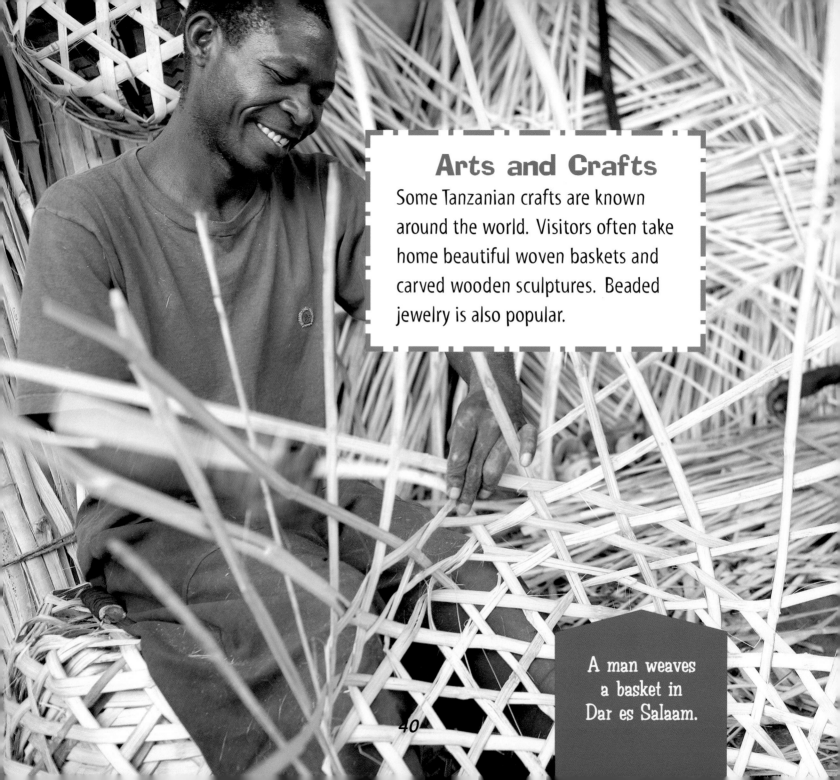

Arts and Crafts

Some Tanzanian crafts are known around the world. Visitors often take home beautiful woven baskets and carved wooden sculptures. Beaded jewelry is also popular.

A man weaves a basket in Dar es Salaam.

40

Printed cotton fabrics are another specialty. A *kanga* has a saying or proverb printed on it. It also has a border around the edges. A *kitenge* has a printed design. Women wear them as skirts. Sometimes women twist them to cushion a load on their heads. They can even use them to carry a baby!

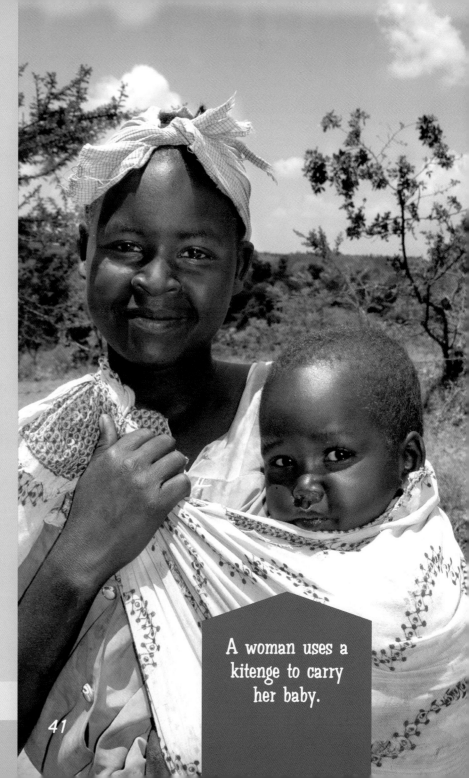

A woman uses a kitenge to carry her baby.

Kick It!

Tanzanians love to play soccer. Kids kick around a ball whenever and wherever they can. People cheer local teams in larger towns and cities. The country is working to improve the national team, the Taifa Stars. They want to get to the World Cup finals.

Tanzania's Kevin Yondani *(left)* goes after the ball alongside Brazil's Luis Fabiano *(center)*.

Tanzanians have already been world champions in distance running. They have won many international marathons. These races are 26 miles (42 km) long!

Tanzania's Phaustin Baha Sulle *(left)* and Christopher Isengwe *(right)* lead in a marathon during the world athletics championships in 2009.

THE FLAG OF TANZANIA

Tanzania's flag features a thick black stripe. It runs from the top right to the bottom left. Black stands for the Tanzanian people. A gold stripe runs along each side of the black stripe. The gold stands for the country's gold and minerals. The flag's top left triangle is green. It stands for the land. The bottom right triangle is blue. It is a symbol of the sea. This design was adopted as the flag of Tanzania after the country united in 1964.

FAST FACTS

FULL COUNTRY NAME: United Republic of Tanzania

AREA: 364,881 square miles (945,037 square kilometers), or a little more than twice the size of California

MAIN LANDFORMS: the Great Rift Valley; the mountains Kilimanjaro and Meru; the volcano Ol Doinyo Lengai; the Central Plateau; the Ngorongoro Crater

MAJOR RIVERS: Rufiji, Ruvuma, Pangani

ANIMALS AND THEIR HABITATS: black rhinos (Ngorongoro Crater); chimpanzees (Gombe Stream National Park); red colobus monkeys (Jozani Forest, Zanzibar); Nile crocodiles and hippopotamuses (riverbanks and lakeshores); antelope, elephants, giraffes, lions, Thomson's gazelles, warthogs, wildebeests, zebras (grassy plains and savannas); hawksbill turtles (Indian Ocean); weavers (throughout)

CAPITAL CITY: Dodoma for lawmakers, Dar es Salaam for the courts and the president. In the future, all government will move to Dodoma.

OFFICIAL LANGUAGES: Swahili and English

POPULATION: about 41,048,500

GLOSSARY

ancestors: relatives who lived long ago

continent: any one of seven large areas of land. The continents are Africa, Antarctica, Asia, Australia, Europe, North America, and South America.

crater: a bowl-shaped pit covering a mountain or a volcano

culture: the way of life, ideas, and customs of a particular group of people

ethnic group: a group of people that shares many things in common, such as customs, religion, history, and language

map: a drawing or chart of all or part of Earth or the sky

plateau: an area of high, flat land

safari: a trip to see animals in the wild, usually in eastern Africa

Swahili time: the system of time used in Tanzania. It counts the hours since sunrise or sunset.

valley: an area of low ground between hills, mountains, or other higher ground

volcano: an opening in Earth's surface through which hot, melted rock and ash sometimes shoot out

TO LEARN MORE

BOOKS

Douglas, Susan. *Ramadan.* Minneapolis: Millbrook Press, 2004. Learn about the history and customs of this important Muslim holiday.

Krensky, Stephen. *The Lion and the Hare: An East African Folktale.* Minneapolis: Millbrook Press, 2009. Enjoy this East African folktale about a mean lion and a clever hare.

Markle, Sandra. *Lions.* Minneapolis: Lerner Publications Company, 2005. This book gets up close to one of Tanzania's fiercest hunters.

Nabwire, Constance, and Bertha Vining Montgomery. *Cooking the East African Way.* Minneapolis: Lerner Publications Company, 2002. This book has recipes for several dishes from the area around Tanzania.

WEBSITES

PBS: AFRICA—Africa for Kids—Swahili Folktale
http://pbskids.org/africa/php/tale.php

Tanzania—FactMonster.com
http://www.factmonster.com/ipka/A0108028.html

Time for Kids: Homework Helper—Around the World—Tanzania
http://www.timeforkids.com/TFK/kids/hh/goplaces/main/0,28375,1585165,00.html

INDEX